Updike ARP

Wednesday Analyzy Mathulda's Character
3 Characteristic 5 Paragraphs.
Intro
A.
B.
C.
Conclusion

The Necklace

CHARLES TOMLINSON

The Necklace

LONDON
OXFORD UNIVERSITY PRESS
NEW YORK TORONTO
1966

Oxford University Press, Ely House, London W. 1

GLASGOW NEW YORK TORONTO MELBOURNE WELLINGTON
CAPE TOWN SALISBURY IBADAN NAIROBI LUSAKA ADDIS ABABA
BOMBAY CALCUTTA MADRAS KARACHI LAHORE DACCA
KUALA LUMPUR HONG KONG

First published by the Fantasy Press
at Swinford, Eynsham, Oxford, 1955

PRINTED IN GREAT BRITAIN
AT THE UNIVERSITY PRESS, OXFORD
BY VIVIAN RIDLER
PRINTER TO THE UNIVERSITY

TO JUSTINE AND JULIET

AUTHOR'S PREFACE

IT is ten years now since *The Necklace* first appeared. Donald Davie's generous recognition of it gave one the courage to go on 'realizing', as Cézanne has it, 'one's little sensation'. The conditions of the realization lay in according objects their own existence. This was what complicated the debt to Wallace Stevens: the poems were both a dialogue with and a departure from him. *The Art of Poetry*, for instance, its third verse playfully modelled on *The Snow Man*, demurs about certain aspects of Stevensian 'elegance'; the according of things their own life demurs about Stevens's insistence on 'the supreme fiction'. All this was done, I hope, lightly. Stevens's sense of the complex relation of observer and environment fascinated me, but was there ever a poetry which stood so explicitly by a physical universe and against transcendence, but which gives so little account of that universe, its spaces, patterns, textures, 'a world of canon and fugue', such as Hopkins spoke of seeing before him?

I trust that this new edition of *The Necklace* will meet the needs of those many people who have written to me in search of a book whose original printing has long since been exhausted.

CHARLES TOMLINSON

Ozleworth Bottom, 1966

ACKNOWLEDGEMENTS

ACKNOWLEDGEMENTS are due to the Editors of the following periodicals in which certain of these poems first appeared: *The Adelphi, Checker, Poetry Chicago*, and *Shenandoah*.

CONTENTS

The necklace is a carving not a kiss
WALLACE STEVENS

INTRODUCTION

THESE poems require no introduction. From one point of view this is the most astonishing thing about them, the way they build up for themselves their own poetic universe. And if the world they inhabit is conspicuously 'their own', it is not therefore a private world. On the contrary; we are offered here no private symbolism or *ad hoc* mythology, no projection of conflicts personal to the poet. The world of these poems is a public one, open to any man who has kept clean and in order his nervous sensitivity to the impact of shape and mass and colour, odour, texture, and timbre. The poems appeal outside of themselves only to the world perpetually bodied against our senses. They improve that world. Once we have read them, it appears to us renovated and refreshed, its colours more delicate and clear, its masses more momentous, its sounds and odours sharper, more distinct. Nothing could be less literary, less amenable to discussion in terms of schools and influences.

But it is just this, perhaps, that to one sort of reader will be a difficulty. We are so used, some of us, to taking our bearings from literature that we are at a loss without them. To such readers one might offer one or two suggestions.

Like most considerable poets of the past thirty years or more, Charles Tomlinson has taken note of the experiments and achievements of French symbolism. This does not mean that he belongs to the post-symbolist 'school' or the post-symbolist 'movement', if there are such things. For my own part I find that I need to remember only one aspect of symbolism, and that an easy one, Rimbaud's 'dérèglement de tous les sens':

> The glare of brass over a restless bass
> (Red glow across olive twilight)

There is nothing recondite in this. Was it not Gustav Holst who composed a suite of musical pieces, each to render the quality of a particular colour? And we all know that a vulgar tie is 'loud', that when a woman wears a purple hat with a green coat, the colours 'shout' at each other. In many of these poems the central artifice is as simple as that; and it can be understood and accepted without knowing anything about Rimbaud at all. It is a familiar phenomenon of all human perception, and it is an artifice only in the sense that the poet takes this most natural phenomenon and refines upon it.

For of course the lines just quoted present the phenomenon only in its simplest form. The clue once given, the poet elaborates upon it. And in its subtler manifestations, it may go unnoticed unless we are prepared for it. For instance the poem called *Nine Variations in a Chinese Winter Setting* is no piece of fashionable chinoiserie. Nor has it anything to do with translations from the Chinese by Arthur Waley or Ezra Pound. It is an exercise in rendering the perceptions of one sense by vocabulary drawn from the others:

> Pine-scent
> In snow-clearness
> Is not more exactly counterpointed
> Than the creak of trodden snow
> Against a flute.

Scent and sight and sound flow together. And I have already falsified. For it is not after all a question of describing scent or sight in terms of sound, as in the first example where 'glare of brass' equals 'red glow' (and note, even here, that it is *glare* of brass, not *blare*). Rather, what emerges from the stanza is not scent or sound or sight, but a quality that is all of these and none of them, that comes to life only when all of them, each in its own rich identity, come into perception together.

What is more, the poet can arrange the properties as he pleases. By arranging together pines, snow, walking feet, flutes, and a particular sort of light, or raffia, bow-strings, bows, bats, winds, bamboos, and flutes (his fourth variation) he creates a sound, a scent, a sight, and a peculiar atmosphere compounded of these, that 'never was on sea or land'. And this again (not that it matters) is an elaboration of the symbolist 'paysage interieur'.

The poet can go further. For there is another essential component of the 'paysage'—the observer, the apparatus that records the impacts made upon it by the senses. The sense and sounds, and the atmosphere compounded of these, will vary with the nature of the thing that responds to them. Bats hear sounds pitched too high for the ear of man, dogs smell what we cannot. The asdic transforms shape and mass into sound. Hence we can imagine a peculiar cast of mind, or a magic glass, or an apparatus of a special sort; and having imagined these, we can deduce with a sort of logic the world that this mind would perceive, or that this machine would render for our inspection.

This is what happens in the difficult poem *Dialogue*, where the thing discussed may be the mind of an artist, or a sort of radar-cum-convex mirror-cum-X-ray. As we deduce the mind of a painter from his vision of the world rendered upon canvas, so we deduce the nature of this thing from the sort of world it presents for our inspection. The logic works both ways.

Again, if one requires a precedent, it can be found, in the poet who supplies an epigraph, and something more to this volume, the American poet, Wallace Stevens. Tomlinson having found an image for the sea, remarks,

A static instance therefore untrue,

for the world changes perpetually before our eyes, and no sooner have we recorded our momentary perceptions than they are proved false. Wallace Stevens, in his *Sea Surface full of Clouds*, shows how the sea alters, not only with alterations in the sky above it and the sea-floor beneath it, but with changes in the climate of our mood as we perceive it. And a later poem by Stevens, *Thirteen Ways of Looking at a Blackbird*, passes, as Tomlinson does in his *Dialogue*, from observation to constructive hypothesis. The way we look at blackbirds depends on the circumstances in which they appear, circumstances which include the sort of people we are, and the sort of mood we are in. We can construct a set of circumstances; and however unlikely these are ('He rode over Connecticut In a glass coach') we can deduce by the logic of imagination how blackbirds would appear in those circumstances.

This poem by Stevens has suggested, I think, the form employed by Tomlinson in his *Eight Observations on the Nature of Eternity* and *Nine Variations in a Chinese Winter Setting*. A title like *Suggestions for the Improvement of a Sunset* similarly recalls titles used by Stevens. So it is just as well to point out that what we have here is no slavish imitation, conscious or unconscious pastiche. Stevens has been a model certainly; but he has not been allowed to dictate, to overpower the different vision of the poet who has learned from him. It would be truer to say that this poet has chosen to develop one side of Stevens, the side represented by *Thirteen Ways of Looking at a Blackbird*.

For the effect of reading these poems is quite unlike the effect of reading a volume by Stevens. It is even more unlike the effect of such other poets as Keats and Tennyson, who are both concerned in their different ways, as this poet is, to

xiv

register sense-perceptions with exquisite precision. The effect of these poems is anything but languorous or hectic or opulent. On the contrary they are taut, bare, and alert. This is largely a matter of versification. There are many kinds of free-verse: Charles Tomlinson's, I think, is designed to keep out of his poetry all effects as of surging violins and insistent drum-beats. One finds one's self compelled to use his vocabulary, to talk of one sense in terms of another, one art in terms of the other arts. His verse is musical; it is euphonious, and it sets up rhythms which are interesting and memorable. But these rhythms are curt, they stop short at just the point where they might become powerful and intoxicating. It is this that gives the effect of alertness and chastity. At its best, this poetry reminds us of what the musician means by 'phrasing'; in the blank spaces on the page, at the end of each line, after each comma or full-stop, the sound of what we have just heard goes on echoing in the mind. The poet expresses this himself in the recurrent image of the flute; for the most part he is writing an unaccompanied melody for the flute, where Stevens and Keats and Tennyson use the whole orchestra.

Diction and versification go together:

> There must be nothing
> Superfluous, nothing which is not elegant
> And nothing which is if it is merely that.

This is more than Stevens could say, and more than he would want to say. In *Sea Surface full of Clouds* there is a great deal that is elegant for its own sake. And this is all very well for Stevens, who declares himself a Romantic, prizing excess in human behaviour as in human language. But Tomlinson is vowed to the flute:

> The glare of brass over a restless bass
> (Red glow across olive twilight)
> Urges to a delighted excess,
> A weeping among broken gods.
>
> The flute speaks (reason's song
> Riding the ungovernable wave)
> The bound of passion
> Out of the equitable core of peace.

xv

In *Through Binoculars* we learn that 'Binoculars are the last phase in a romanticism', from which the poet returns with relief to 'normality'. And in *Observation of Facts*, elegance is merely 'frippery' until it incorporates 'mental fibre', like 'a rough pot or two' introduced into a too feminine room. Tomlinson's morality is sternly traditional, classical, almost Augustan. If he had not chosen to make this explicit, we could still have inferred it from the dryness and reticence of his art, its addiction to the bleak contour, to terse understatement and brief energetic rhythms. Just because he is as far as possible from a hedonist or Art-for-Art's-Saker, the pleasures of sensuous perception, as we gather them from his poems, never cloy or go stale on the tongue through over-indulgence.

I end as I began. These poems present analysis of human perception, how it works and how it ought to work, in a healthy personality. But the proof of the pudding is in the eating, the proof of the analysis is in the buoyant health of the poet's own perceptions, their crispness, the inevitability of the phrasing he finds for them:

> The scene terminates without words
> A tower collapsing upon feathers . . .

> The sea-voice
> Tearing the silence from the silence . . .

I have derived, and I still derive, enormous pleasure from these poems. So will others, I am sure.

DONALD DAVIE

AESTHETIC

REALITY is to be sought, not in concrete,
But in space made articulate:
The shore, for instance,
Spreading between wall and wall;
The sea-voice
Tearing the silence from the silence.

VENICE

CUT into by doors
The morning assumes night's burden,
The houses assemble in tight cubes.

From the palace flanking the waterfront
She is about to embark, but pauses.
Her dress is a veil of sound
Extended upon silence.

Under the bridge,
Contained by the reflected arc
A tunnel of light
Effaces walls, water, horizon.

Floating upon its own image
A cortège of boats idles through space.

NINE VARIATIONS
IN A CHINESE WINTER SETTING

I

WARM flute on the cold snow
Lays amber in sound.

II

Against brushed cymbal
Grounds yellow on green,
Amber on tinkling ice.

III

The sage beneath the waterfall
Numbers the blessing of a flute;
Water lets down
Exploding silk.

IV

The hiss of raffia,
The thin string scraped with the back of the bow
Are not more bat-like
Than the gusty bamboos
Against a flute.

V

Pine-scent
In snow-clearness
Is not more exactly counterpointed
Than the creak of trodden snow
Against a flute.

VI

The outline of the water-dragon
Is not embroidered with so intricate a thread
As that with which the flute
Defines the tangible borders of a mood.

VII

The flute in summer makes streams of ice:
In winter it grows hospitable.

VIII

In mist, also, a flute is cold
Beside a flute in snow.

IX

Degrees of comparison
Go with differing conditions:
Sunlight mellows lichens,
Whereas snow mellows the flute.

EIGHT OBSERVATIONS
ON THE NATURE OF ETERNITY

I

You would not think the room
(Grown small as a honey pot
And filled with a slow yellow light)
Could so burden itself with the afternoon.

II

It is neither between three and four
Nor is it time for the lamps:
It is afternoon—interminably.

III

Elsewhere there is sky, movement or a view,
Here there is light, stillness and no dimension.

IV

The afternoon violet
Is not so unthinkably itself,
Nor does that imperceptibly greening light
Freeze so remotely in its own essence
As this yellow.

V

Red flowers
Detonate and go out
At the curtain fringe.

VI

Objects regard us for the last time,
The window, that enemy of solitude,
Looks inward.

VII

Jaws of unhurried shade
Yawn on the masonry.

VIII

We will light no candles:
What is to be will be.
The room is merging
Into a moonless landscape.

SUGGESTIONS FOR THE
IMPROVEMENT OF A SUNSET

DARKENING the edges of the land,
Imperceptibly it must drain out colours
Drawing all light into its centre.

Six points of vantage provide us with six sunsets.

The sea partakes of the sky. It is less
Itself than the least pool which, if threatened,
Prizes lucidity.

The pond is lime-green, an enemy
Of gold, bearing no change but shadow.

Seen from above, the house would resemble
A violin, abandoned, and lost in its own darkness;

Diminished, through the wrong end of a glass,
A dice ambushed by lowering greens;

Accorded its true proportions,
The stone would give back the light
Which, all day, it has absorbed.

The after-glow, broken by leaves and windows,
Confirms green's triumph against yellow.

SEA CHANGE

To define the sea—
We change our opinions
With the changing light.

Light struggles with colour:
A quincunx
Of five stones, a white
Opal threatened by emeralds.

The sea is uneasy marble.

The sea is green silk.

The sea is blue mud, churned
By the insistence of wind.

Beneath dawn a sardonyx may be cut from it
In white layers laced with a carnelian orange,
A leek- or apple-green chalcedony
Hewn in the cold light.

Illustration is white wine
Floating in a saucer of ground glass
On a pedestal of cut glass:

A static instance, therefore untrue.

THROUGH BINOCULARS

In their congealed light
We discover that what we had taken for a face
Has neither eyes nor mouth,
But only the impersonality of anatomy.

Silencing movement,
They withdraw life.

Definition grows clear-cut, but bodiless,
Withering by a dimension.

To see thus
Is to ignore the revenge of light on shadow,
To confound both in a brittle and false union.

This fictive extension into madness
Has a kind of bracing effect:
That normality is, after all, desirable
One can no longer doubt having experienced its opposite.

Binoculars are the last phase in a romanticism:
The starkly mad vision, not mortal,
But dangling one in a vicarious, momentary idiocy.

To dispense with them
Is to make audible the steady roar of evening,
Withdrawing in slow ripples of orange,
Like the retreat of water from sea-caves.

MONTAGE

The cheval-glass is empty
The sky is a blank screen.

In the buried room
They look back upon themselves.

The comity of three objects
Builds stillness within stillness.

The scene terminates without words
A tower collapsing upon feathers.

DIALOGUE

She: It turns on its axis.

He: To say that it was round
      Would be to ignore what is within:
      The transparent framework of cells,
      The constellation of flashes.

She: It reveals the horizon.

He: It surrounds it,
      Transmits and refines it
      Through a frozen element:
      A taut line crossing a pure white.

She: It contains distance.

He: It distances what is near,
      Transforms the conversation piece
      Into a still life,
      Isolates, like the end of a corridor.

She: It is the world of contour:

He: The black outline separating brilliances
      That would otherwise fuse,
      A single flame.

She: If it held personages—

He: They would be minute,
      Their explicit movements
      The mosaic which dances.

Both: In unison, they would clarify
      The interior of the fruit,
      The heart of the cut stone.

FLUTE MUSIC

There is a moment for speech and for silence.
Lost between possibilities
But deploring a forced harmony,
We elect the flute.

A season, defying gloss, may be the sum
Of blue water beneath green rain;
It may comprise comets, days, lakes
Yet still bear the exegesis of music.

Seeing and speaking we are two men:
The eye encloses as a window—a flute
Governs the land, its winter and its silence.

The flute is uncircumscribed by moonlight or irised
        mornings.
It moves with equal certainty
Through a register of palm-greens and flesh-rose.

The glare of brass over a restless bass
(Red glow across olive twilight)
Urges to a delighted excess,
A weeping among broken gods.

The flute speaks (reason's song
Riding the ungovernable wave)
The bound of passion
Out of the equitable core of peace.

THE BEAD

At the clear core, morning
Extinguishes everything save light.

Breaking the spectrum
Threads cross, flare, emerge
Like the glitter of dust before stained windows.

Turned in the shadow
It is a black diamond
Containing nothing but itself.

The idea dissolves in passion:
The light holds,
Circling the cold centre.

THE DEATH OF THE INFANTA

for Donald Davie

OUTSIDE, upon warm air,
The impingement of strollers and public flowers.

Between the cold walls
You would say that space, also, was stone.

The perspective hollows itself into the distance
Littered with chairs and statues.

Her room you would suppose
The ultimate box held by the others,
Her person, the final space.

But you would err. Her glass
Catches the finale of both.

At first, the mind feels bruised.
The light makes white holes through the black foliage
Or mist hides everything that is not itself.

But how shall one say so?—
The fact being, that when the truth is not good enough
We exaggerate. Proportions

Matter. It is difficult to get them right.
There must be nothing
Superfluous, nothing which is not elegant
And nothing which is if it is merely that.

This green twilight has violet borders.

Yellow butterflies
Nervously transferring themselves
From scarlet to bronze flowers
Disappear as the evening appears.

OBSERVATION OF FACTS

FACTS have no eyes. One must
Surprise them, as one surprises a tree
By regarding its (shall I say?)
Facets of copiousness.

The tree stands.

The house encloses.

The room flowers.

These are fact stripped of imagination:
Their relation is mutual.

A dryad is a sort of chintz curtain
Between myself and a tree.
The tree stands: or does not stand:
As I draw, or remove the curtain.

The house encloses: or fails to signify
As being bodied over against one,
As something one has to do with.

The room flowers once one has introduced
Mental fibre beneath its elegance,
A rough pot or two, outweighing
The persistence of frippery
In lampshades or wallpaper.

Style speaks what was seen,
Or it conceals the observation
Behind the observer: a voice
Wearing a ruff.

Those facets of copiousness which I proposed
Exist, do so when we have silenced ourselves.

FIASCHERINO

OVER an ash-fawn beach fronting a sea which keeps
 Rolling and unrolling, lifting
The green fringes from submerged rocks
 On its way in, and, on its way out
Dropping them again, the light

Squanders itself, a saffron morning
 Advances among foam and stones, sticks
Clotted with black naphtha
 And frayed to the newly carved
Fresh white of chicken flesh.

One leans from the cliff-top. Height
 Distances like an inverted glass; the shore
Is diminished but concentrated, jewelled
 With the clarity of warm colours
That, seen more nearly, would dissipate

Into masses. The map-like interplay
 Of sea-light against shadow
And the mottled close-up of wet rocks
 Drying themselves in the hot air
Are lost to us. Content with our portion,

Where, we ask ourselves, is the end of all this
 Variety that follows us? Glare
Pierces muslin; its broken rays
 Hovering in trembling filaments
Glance on the ceiling with no more substance

Than a bee's wing. Thickening, these
 Hang down over the pink walls
In green bars, and, flickering between them,
 A moving fan of two colours,
The sea unrolls and rolls itself into the low room.